W9-AUJ-516

deciduous qween

deciduous qween

poems

Matty Layne Glasgow

Red Hen Press | *Pasadena, CA*

Book design by Mark E. Cull

Library of Congress Cataloging-in-Publication Data

Names: Glasgow, Matty Layne.
Title: Deciduous qween : poems / Matty Layne Glasgow.
Other titles: Deciduous queen
Description: First edition. | Pasadena, CA : Red Hen Press, 2019.
Identifiers: LCCN 2018056199 | ISBN 9781597092586 (tradebook)
Classification: LCC PS3607.L3585 D43 2019 | DDC 811/.6—dc23
LC record available at https://lccn.loc.gov/2018056199

The National Endowment for the Arts, the Los Angeles County Arts Commis-
sion, the Ahmanson Foundation, the Dwight Stuart Youth Fund, the Max Fac-
tor Family Foundation, the Pasadena Tournament of Roses Foundation, the Pas-
adena Arts & Culture Commission and the City of Pasadena Cultural Affairs
Division, the City of Los Angeles Department of Cultural Affairs, the Audrey
& Sydney Irmas Charitable Foundation, the Kinder Morgan Foundation, the
Allergan Foundation, and the Riordan Foundation partially support Red Hen
Press.

First Edition
Published by Red Hen Press
www.redhen.org

ACKNOWLEDGMENTS

Kind thanks to the readers & editors of the following publications who provided homes for early versions of these poems:

BOAAT: "Hot Shit"; *Cosmonauts Avenue*: "bodyslam glam"; *Crazyhorse*: "Elegy for Honeybee"; *Ecotone*: "reprise"; *Front Porch Journal*: "the power(bottom) is yours"; *Frontier Poetry*: "deciduous qween, IV" & "For Ayotzinapa"; *Grist*: "Pando" & "Quaking Aspen, or dendrophilia"; *Houston Public Media*: "Hippocampus, or If I were a boy"; *Indolent Books (HIV Here & Now)*: "haiku for my first boyfriend on his twenty-eighth birthday"; *Muzzle Magazine*: "Texas was a time that never moved"; *Nimrod*: "Ash Mama" & "Plumage"; *Oxidant Engine*: "grounded" & "How to be strong"; *Puerto del Sol*: "cactus mouth, or *opuntia macrocentra kush*," "Jazz June," & "boundary // fluidity" (appeared as "My body lies"); *RATTLE (Poets Respond)*: "What the Mountains are Silent About"; *Rust + Moth*: "malignant"; *The Blueshift Journal*: "Mama said funny things"; *The Collagist*: "Silly Goose"; *The Fourth River (Tributaries)*: "Beaver as Fairy Drag Mother"; *The Missouri Review*: "deciduous qween, I," "deciduous qween, II," "deciduous qween, III," "deciduous qween, V," "Bayou Baby"; *The New Verse News*: "make-believe queen bees" (appeared as "make-believe queen bey"); *The Shore*: "Lady Caribou is a Badass"; *Underblong*: "All Afternoon"; *Yes Poetry*: "I grew up wanting"; *Wildness Journal*: "aurora."

A very special thanks to Debra Marquart & Ned Balbo for their tireless generosity in bringing discipline, life, & love to these poems. I'm also grateful for the following friends, poets, & editors for their various roles & kind support along this journey: Sara Cooper, Autumn Hayes, Jack McBride, Long Chu, Robin Reagler, Eliza Hamilton-Poore, Ebonesiah Morrow, Laura Hitt, Phoebe Wagner, Jenna Mertz, Shane Griffin, Brontë Weiland, Molly Backes, Samantha Futhey, Ana Hurtado, Emily Horner, Renee Christopher, Zachary Lisabeth, Taylor Brorby, Camille Meyers, Kristen Daily, Mallory Gunther, Xavier Cavazos, Sonia Marie del Hierro, Jennifer L. Knox, Kate Gale, Jane Satterfield, Heidi Seaborn, David Zimmerman, sam sax, Matthew Sivils, Bonar Hernández, Chloe Clarke, Peter LaBerge, Chen Chen, Josh Roark, Sam Herschel Wein, Taenum Bambrick, Lisbeth White, Anni Liu, Amber Flora Thomas, Elizabeth Giorgi, Kelly Slivka, Eduardo C. Corral, Maggie Smith, & Richard Blanco.

Most importantly, I'd like to thank my mother, father, brother, & Irán, whose unbounded love for & belief in me kept me here.

for Mama

CONTENTS

I

II

III

I

deciduous qween, I

of teeth, being shed at the end of a period of growth

I forget how sharpness first emerged
                              from my jaw
            the way milk teeth pushed
            through tender flesh
                        how they scratched   then chewed
    the insides of my cheeks
                  just to tear another part of me   raw.
                        I forget the taste of blood
            a toddler's iron
on a toddler's tongue
                  the guttural scream of a small creature
      whose only language   was pain.

                  You remember.   Tell me
    no toddler ever teethed with such indignation
                        tell me   *your mama and I just wanted you*
            to be happy   to be quiet.   But your baby
just grew louder and louder   into a gaudy
                  and ungodly thing
                        losing incisors and molars
        like enamel sequins   shedding canines
        keen and shiny as plastic diamonds.
                        They'd all fall
            out of my mouth   like sighs
so high-pitched   they shimmered
                        in glitter-dusted confetti.

This is how I learned to sell my body
                              one tooth at a time
        for a quarter   then a dollar
and you'd hold all the smallest parts of me
                        in your hand   glistening white
        opal stones unearthed   from my gums
                        like words that only shine

when they are free from the dark caverns
   of my unmuzzled maw.
      This is how I learned to let go
   for a price
     those blood-stained roots
      the only soft, dangling remnants
of loss.

Texas was a time that never moved

I came from a pearl of sweat that fell
from Mama's brow on a Texas day in
August. Texas was a time that never moved
forward. August was scorched earth & steam—
a thick haze that swayed over the pavement.
When that pearl fell through flame & burst,
I danced pretty for Mama & Daddy
& whoever else would watch, just to keep
my feet from roasting on the coals. Texas is still
an unsetting sun; it hangs in time, forgets
the bodies it's hanged & burned & buried.
August is a boy ablaze—cheeks flushed full
of fire, his feet aflicker. But I learned to burn
the past on my arms & carry it with me.

Silly Goose

I recently drew a map of my childhood:
a cul-de-sac on the edge of a great lake,
a bench beneath an old oak, a feath-
er-dusted shoreline where I craved more
than breadcrumbs or confit de canard.
One summer night, I held stale bread
between my fingers, like crusted sand-
paper so dry mallards & geese quacked
bitch, please! Squawked *hell, naw!*
Until Mama's scream pierced the flut-
ter of feathers, & I saw a pair of white
wings spread wide & shimmer in the
streetlamp. The goose lowered his head,
& his bristled beak tore right through
her pantyhose. I remember how every-
thing fell in the shadows—handfuls of
bread on the grass, Mama's blood drip-
ping from her calf to the shore's plum-
age. It's strange how things that belong
somewhere else always seem so violent
out of place, like soft, wingless feathers
or a hunger for the wrong kind of flesh.

grounded

at seven, I learned
the law of gravity:
eyes pulled down-

ward to feathers
to wings splayed up-
on the grass & fire-

dusted chest to sky
like ants all aflame
in those empty eyes,

& when I fell I saw
the clouds beneath
my feet. how the

world refused to stay
in place. it still falls &
crawls where it does

not belong—in hills,
in mounds fashioned
of feather & bone.

Boy Vultures in Love

A Gay Vulture Couple . . . at the Artis Zoo in Amsterdam recently
welcomed a chick after taking in an abandoned egg in their aviary unit.
—A Gay Couple Hatched a Chick Together: "They Proved They Can,"
Time, June 1, 2017

Male vultures are known as sporks,
which is to say these two are versatile
in the nest, scavengers in the sack who

make it work with what they've found
in one another. They were the only ones
who saw the egg on the feathered floor

of that aviary & understood what it meant
to be unwanted by one's mother, or father,
even if just for a moment—slow caress of

unbroken shell abandoned on soft plumage.
Those two lovebirds built a nest
of scavenged twigs & hopeless longing.

The news articles called them *gay*, said
they proved they can, as though there were
ever any doubt. What is that word to birds

of prey anyway? I'm told they speak Dutch
there, so really they're homoseksueel, or just
two boy vultures in love, their zonderling days

all await for larger beasts to fall, curved beaks
ready to carve any carrion rife & ripe from long
afternoons steeped in summer heat. All await

for an unhatched life, feathers eager & ruffling
for a beak to crack the warmth of a fathered shell—
its halved emptiness the only thing forsaken.

bodyslam glam

for Cassandro & all the queer exóticos

Papá always counted to three before he'd lay a hand on me. The sharp stench of tequila slipping through his lips, no slur in his warning just yet. *Uno . . . dos . . . tres.* & after those four syllables, en su borrachera, the hands that drove his truck & turned that wheel left on my ass palms full of lavender, of lilac. I felt the pain bloom from my body like a garden that grew along with me. I wore the work of his fists & palms like a sundress, sitting in math class, mouthing my own emptiness—hollowed numbers—as los niños y las niñas contaron in a slow drone: *uno . . . dos . . . tres.* My petals throbbed & stung & shivered with each recitation. & outside on the playground, I learned to play patty cake, patty cake with a boy like me, to press my palms into his & never leave a flower behind. Now,

I live in the shadows of my own glitter-dusted eyes, wear purple shimmer like a veil because I grew tired of trying to fight from behind a mask. I love the spandex, too—shades of lavender that glimmer like a bruise beneath the lights. Tights that palm my waist & round ass like cling wrap as I strut to the ring, squat, & slip between the ropes that bend & pull & stretch, like our faith when the ones we love most let us down. But some ropes aren't meant to hang or bind, rather to bring someone back to us with more force. Preferably a burly masked luchador, himself half-naked & oiled up, so I can take him in my arms, lift him overhead, & throw him down on the mat. I want to cover all the strongest luchas with my bodyslam glam in a hot mist of purple glitter to the crowd chanting *uno . . . dos . . . tres.* & beneath the tights, my body still blooms.

Elegy for Honeybee

We were intimate once.

You plunged yourself into my young purlicue,
left your stinger & insides behind & split—
the day's damp sheath spilling behind you.
I watched you leave, fierce & aflutter, gold
spiraling into darkness.

I was a child then,

listening to my pulse with each throb, listening
to your flight—a broken bow along a string
of wind. I wanted to wear your dissonance,
to shroud myself in the yellow sequins & black
leather of a gaudy drag ensemble, so you'd know

I was broken, too.

I never told you I loved the way you pierced
the soft flesh of my body, how you filled the space
between my fingers with a pain I learned to pinch
more & more pleasure from. Now,

absence is the quiet of your wings,

their soft sputter in drifting mists & avarice.
Your poison-soaked bodice, flaxen blackened,
writhes on the branch of an almond tree.
My regret is the pinprick scar I no longer feel.
There's a buzz in the air.

It's the world unzipping:

almond tree bare, petals sapped of their pigment.
I wilt in their gray perfume—an older, bitter qween
stitching together frayed costumes of younger days,
when I'd wear the leaves & flowers you left me.
I'm still here, unraveling your sacrifice in the hand

                    that could never keep you.

Mama said funny things

while she was dying, and the dying didn't take long.
Like when some lady who ran a nonprofit for people

who were dying too young sent her a basket of stuff,
she said *What do I need all this shit for now?* She pulled

out the little Bible and said *I don't have time to read,
I just wanna do do do.* Holding some plastic inflatable

thing, she hissed *What the hell is this?* And she threw
that little amorphous ball at me, round like her belly

because all that fluid just had no place else to go.
There we sat on the floor together, riffling through

that dumb shit like little kids, throwing it all across
the bedroom. We laughed and laughed, until it hurt.

Mama said funny things while she was dying,
and sometimes it sounded like a song. Like when

we went to the emergency room and she asked
Am I still an emergency, baby boy? I said I'd always

turn the sirens on for her. And as she lay there
on the hospital bed while that poor nurse couldn't

find a damn vein, Mama asked *What does triage mean
anyway?* I said it's a place where there's lots of blood.

She said *Well we certainly don't have that problem in here,
do we, baby?* And we giggled, and my daddy

and my brother laughed, too, and they laughed until
that laughter found a vein, and their eyes broke, and

their eyes bled like a dam. They just bled and bled
until it hurt and they thought they'd never bleed again.

⌁

Mama said funny things while she was dying,
but she was funny all along. I remember four days

before all that funny breath left her forever, how
Daddy had been watching the Ryder Cup in the living

room with his sister and my brother and me all
weekend. Mama needed help from the bed to the toilet

and back, so I wrapped my arm around her and shuffled
real slow because it all just seemed to be going too fast.

She asked *Are they still in there watching fucking golf?*
I told her no, that it was all over now, and she said

Oh thank god, baby boy. It's not even a sport, is it? I laughed,
and I said no, Mama, it's not even a fucking sport.

It's nothing. You could do it in your sleep. She said *Well,
I'll have plenty of time for that then, won't I, baby?* I laughed

and laughed until I felt like I'd never laugh again. She held
me in her arms and said *Baby boy, I'm so scared. I'm so so scared.*

II

deciduous qween, II

of antlers, being shed at the end of a period of growth

There were two crowns. I wore them both
like a pair of antlers—diamond-encrusted
bone that began to grow from my pedicles
when I was four, prancing about our living
room in a Mickey Mouse onesie, doing the
pretty dance on baby qween's first stage—
a shaggy carpet—twirling for baby qween's
first audience: Mama & Daddy & Brother.
That afternoon, I felt sparkling silver gleam
sprout from my skull like all my bones were
precious metal, & I just wanted to let them
shine, to let anyone hold my body in the light
so I could look like I was worth something.
It took twenty years for the first coronation,
for those fairy drag mothers to pin diamond
& metal into my cheap wig. It took one year
to let go, to pass that crown along to another
qween like an omen, like the outline of a buck
in headlights—his head tipped back, his eyes
lost in the night sky as he braces for some sort
of impact. Sometimes I want to be crushed
by an oilfield tanker on a road carved from
west Texas dirt, somewhere between Ozona
& Big Lake & Garden City, but I haven't
really thought about it. Sometimes, I want to
be manhandled by an applause—the force of
hand against hand channeled into my bones
so fiercely cracks spider my crowns' metallic
stems until they shatter. I'll grind what's left
into silver buds, smoke my reign into ash, feel
those bone-fleshed flames fill my lungs. Maybe
I'll always wear my royalty on the inside, take
a drag or a hit & hold onto that high because
I learned nothing lasts, least of all an unloved

body. I've met too many men who don't want
the crown so much as the head it rests upon.
So let them take that, too. I'd give up all my
bones just to know they're still worth wanting.

pedicles,
  or this is where

every antler is an adolescence
that sheds its vascular skin—bloodied

velvet scraped like childhood against
a red maple's trunk. Call it ritual—

how you leave that tenderness on
the forest floor for these hardened,

honeycombed bones ephemerally
fastened to your skull. How your

flesh softens as your testosterone
begins to fade, and you remember

what it is to be more fawn than buck,
to feel that sharpness weigh on your

head and body like a shame that weakens
the blood. I am those heavy antlers;

this is where I leave you—between
eyes of burnt umber and soft salt-

and-pepper-furred ears. You'll learn
to seduce without a crown, to survive

without a weapon—hide soaked in
your will to grow and grow and

Lady Caribou is a Badass

Deal with it. How she grows antlers
just like the bulls—soft velvet crowns
that harden into sharp-boned flames.

Zoologists say antlers are weapons
that bulls use to control harems.
Lady Caribou says *I can run my own crew,*

fuckboy, says *I know these antlers ain't*
forever, but I'll show you what I'm made of.
Zoologists say antlers are objects of

sexual attraction. Lady Caribou says
We all want to be wanted, says *We're all*
drawn to the fire. Some zoologists say

Lady Caribou's antlers are smaller &
less complex than a bull's. Most of those
zoologists are men. Lady Caribou says

Fuck you guys, says *I've got a goddamn crown*
on my head & a calf in my belly. Yes, Lady
Caribou wears a crown just like the boys,

except she carries it through winter, even
as a calf stirs within her, even as her body
knows the weight of two lives. When she

lowers her head, two hearts quicken.
She says *This was never just about me, boy,*
says *You don't fuck with a mother or her flame.*

Hippocampus, or If I were a boy

I'd be a seahorse, waiting for an underwater filly
to court me in the salted shade of coral & ocean
jade. Let us begin with a dance: our tails entwined,
ripples of pre-dawn light, how we hold one another

without hands. I'd care for her eggs, receive them
by the thousand in my pouch, & carry them there
for weeks, until the final contraction releases our fry
into an amniotic fluid of green plankton where

they'd swim poorly, but freely. If I were a seahorse,
I wouldn't watch them as I leave to find another
filly, hold her eggs too. But I'm not the kind of boy
who leaves. This body is a pouch that longs to love

a thousand lives, to push them into this reckless sea
& hold them all together, even after they have gone.

Little Queer on the Prairie

Oh prairie, whip out your big
bluestem. Let me watch it grow,
that laurel stalk so flush full of
fiber as it takes form. Come winter

I want to awaken to your golden
rod, your feathery head never
too close to my face. Stem-slap me,
baby. Let me feel you on my cheek.

Spread your seed & conceive of
a sea of bobbing amber tender to
the touch. I know, the white man,
he let you down, aroused you upon

his colonial arrival, left you with
blue balls for roots, then castrated
them. So Superman that bro. Make
him bathe in your second coming.

What the Mountains Are Silent About

In Chechnya . . . [gay men] met dates online in chat rooms . . . which had names like The Village and What the Mountains Are Silent About.
—Andrew E. Kramer, *The New York Times*

In Chechnya, you can watch the Greater
Caucasus mountains rise queerly along
the southern border, like a man newly gone
from this place—disappeared for wanting
wrongly. Some might say his wings are snow-
capped peaks, but I don't believe in angels
or heaven, so I wonder if those mountains
aren't just piles of ash. And if they could
speak to us, would it be in a low whistle
that shivers pine needles like limbs bound
and trembling from the electrical current
pulsing through them? Would they scream,
the kind that musters all its breath from
the tenderized flesh of a violet bruise or
the space where bone fractures into sharp
shards of what once held his body together?
Listen. You can hear his pained cry in your
own closeted dreams. You know the weight
of these mountains, you've always been here
holding your truth deep within like a flesh of
Paleogene rock because if you made a sound,
they'd come for you, they'd make you crumble.

For Ayotzinapa

On September 26, 2014, forty-three students from
the Raúl Isidro Burgos Rural Teachers' College of Ayotzinapa
were detained by local police in Iguala, Guerrero.
They were never seen again.

when you left   i bathed
the baby in the kitchen sink
he turned to ashes in my arms
that's how i learned
to be covered in loss

to wear it   like the black
hood   tied around
your neck, hands bound
to be severed   fingers
plunged into the red soil

your eyes opened to a star-
less night sky   but you
didn't need the sun
      to burn   now i feel
the heat in every sunrise

& look   out the window
to where our State cut you
down, your limbs down, your
trunk & body & leaf blossom
fingers down   heart down

i found it   in the riverbed
char-soaked from a narco
blaze   the kind that smells
like it don't give a fuck like
our State is his   i knew

where to bury you
to make you grow again
so you disappeared once
more   beneath this land
of bone chips & dried flesh

i'd never watched a man
rise   pull himself out
of the earth
body & branches   still
covered in ash   that's how

you learned to live again
i haven't looked out
the window since that day
too afraid   of what
i might see   the way

you stand   rooted in death
& feel the wind blow right
through you   like bullets

boundary // fluidity

Along the shore of the Río Bravo, we watch
the silty current sunder your home from mine—

a slow flow of brown water that cuts through
Santa Elena Canyon. On the opposite bank,

a girl stands in faded gray jeans, her arms drowned
in a bulky poncho, her body breathless beneath

quilted green & red. She sinks into the muddy
shoreline like a dream, eyes tracing the patchwork

of our entwined fingers as we follow the river's edge.
Some things are made to be crossed, some flesh

is meant to tangle. You are a man & I am a man
& we are contained by no boundary on this day.

*For 1,254 miles, the Río Bravo serves as the natural
border between the U.S. state of Texas and Mexico.*

My body lies. I want to love a man, a woman.
I am the girl. I want to be in the arms of another,

taste her, & yearn for the soft-petaled flavor
of truth. I part my lips, but everything going in

& coming out deceives me. My words are muddy,
too soft to rise toward the unforgiving sun like

a canyon wall. Too cold & wet in the shadows of
red rock to be a flame, but all of me needs to flicker.

What is the natural boundary between us? I want
to wade in that water, to feel the current that keeps

me on the southern bank & you on the other side.
I want to drown with all the others who want more.

The vilest carcasses are the floaters. They turn green,
swell up like a balloon, & stink to high heaven.

The girl is a ghost. She is every woman & every man
who ever wanted. Her poncho bleeds until she wears

the gray of her jeans on her flesh, drapes her loss over
her empty chest, sinks & slips away into any soft, cold

earth that will take her. The girl is a ghost. He needs
to be the girl, before she drowned in her own body,

before she understood she was not a girl, but a boy.
This is what it feels like to be trapped. A ghost has no

body, only regret. The girl is a woman, a man. The girl
is a dream. The girl is my dead mother. The girl is.

Since 1998, more than 6,000 migrants have died trying
to cross the border from Mexico into the United States.

What happens the day we can no longer take refuge
in our own hearts? Remember, the will to cross anything

is to wade in one's courage, to trust our flesh-wrapped
bones to cut through the current. Tell me, who guards

the borders of my body? You are the girl on the southern
bank. I am standing alone, toes sinking into the mud

because I want you beside me before the currents quicken
& rise, like those years we can never return to. I want

to trace your frailty with my fingertips, your slender arms
swimming in quilted fabric, to look you in your emerald

eyes, to lay my head upon your hollow chest & squeeze
the life back into you. The girl on the southern bank

is always sinking, always watching the silty current
until it runs dry & we meet once more in the riverbed.

III

deciduous qween, III
of the body, the breath, not permanent; transitory or ephemeral

I can't lie on my back & look at the sky
without trembling—my haunches sunk

into the grass, my mind wondering when
the ground will let go. Call it a universal fear

of what holds us in space. Call it vertigo—
how we are all in constant motion, even

in our stillness. My yoga instructor says
the final pose is the hardest. Play dead.

Pretend you're okay with it. You deserve
this. When my grandfather died, I heard

my mother moan from her bedroom—her
fear all staccato & breathless *no*, her pain

hollowing my body from belly to chest to
throat. What I lost that night was my faith.

I looked up into darkness. I begged the sky
to show me a place I'd never believe in,

to shed the space between us & let me see
the other side of the horizon. I once knew

a fiery woman, her throat so full of death
she couldn't speak a word. She didn't want

the morphine. Shook her head & groaned as
I squeezed the drops under her dry tongue.

I would have swallowed all the pain for her,
let it fill the emptiness my body carried since

I first heard her cry all those years ago &
learned what it meant to be *gone*. I want to

be brave, to say it's not the being gone but
the going that scares me. But it's all of it.

How my bones will shed this flesh while I'm
still wearing it, how what's left will go in flame

or in the ground days after all I see is darkness.
But I'm still looking up into it. I'm not on my

knees, but if there's someplace worth believing
in out there, I'm still begging it to show me.

here & there

A mother in capris sits for a roadside photo.
Her offspring fidget by her sides. They squint
& smile at the sun, at the camera's gaze. They
are children, & then they are giggling pixies

weaving a bed of bluebonnets into tall braided
bulbs of sapphire hair—a wig that unfurls from
a qween's head, crowned with a white bow. They
pinch stems of Indian paintbrush between their

small fingers, give their qween her stage face—
cheeks flush full of cerise petals, bright rouge
lips to match. From a Mexican hat, the shiniest
pixie cinches a waist, makes a body more narrow

than true. Watch a single bloom cascade, a spill
of burgundy over yellow petals toward the earth.
This is the only way they know to make a dress:
with a purple winecup fashioned into a chalice-

shaped bustier, petals curved to sky, supporting
all of their qween's flesh, even what's not there.
They are drunk on colors of renewal, their hues
of navy blue & pink pastels, their golden flowers

sallowed to shades of orange & blood. Now,
I am here, & there is no mother, no smiling sun,
no offspring nor pixies, no color-drunk hillside,
no wildflower vista. Only me, staring at the snow-

sodden horizon. Only this stem of *Castilleja indivisa*
sprouting within my own pixie flesh, ready to paint
this frozen tundra 'til the endless flat bleeds prairie-
fire with the lust & rust of a Texas spring.

reprise

Do you remember the purple crocus,
how he threatened to tear the petals

from his own sepal? I loved that fucking
wildflower, how he stood with his yellow

pistil in hand wanting to bloom all over again,
how the wind proselytized reincarnation

because to blow away as the Earth spins,
as pressures high & low squeeze your petals,

your stems—well, there's just no justice
in that demise, to end on such a gusty whim.

That fear unfolds within me like a field
of violet spring: a petal-less stem all out

of bloom, the gunshot on the prairie, spirit
drifting over the meadow like a hollow echo.

Another qween boy collapsed on a bed
of wildflowers, waiting to rise.

aurora

Through the padlocked window, I watched

a cardinal cut through morning's hot, dewy flesh.

His feathers crimson-soaked in sunrise. Each wing

a freshly sharpened blade. Each high-pitched pulse

of song loosening memory's stitched wound. I saw my

mother's face and a past lover and a dark comedy.

They all ended the same. I remember mourning, waking

to dawn-soaked bandages holding those feathers within

me. I lay curled under the sheets as you sat on the other

side of the bedrails, head in your hands, wondering how

such a soft, feathery thing could make the morning bleed.

cactus mouth,
    or *Opuntia macrocentra kush*

wake, wake
& bake these west
texas cheeks, these
garden city gums

they're so thirsty
to hollow

arid me
terrain me
until I bear
only you
take you in

these lamesa lips
where you bury
your spines
in my sand-fleshed
cheeks—a sore
memory—so purple

prickly pear kush
you wet succulent
you thorny yellow
blossom, this

mouthful didn't come
from some small pot
on a windowsill

it's a wild one
just off an anxious
gravel road where
I'm on my knees

looking as far
as my glazed eyes
can see into
a fearless flatline
horizon

some other
joyous kind of desert

malignant

my words are like my mother's
cells—a bit rebellious & out of
line. how i called a dying woman
crazy.

    rebel is a word
for those who refuse to remain contained
                         by form
                     or body,
       who break lines like bones, watch
     thoughts splinter   & bury themselves
          in the world's flesh.

    a body is a form
of poetry, how certain lines
  like *her eyes, the thirsty green*
       of a West Texas cactus emerge
          from a dying body   of work.

        i want my words to multiply,
to overwhelm the page   spread
  like cancer   so cantankerous,
     to hollow out the pancreas
   of homophobia   until it no longer secretes
         its bile, leaves the carcass
     of the bigot   in its wake—
   bones picked clean by maggots
        & faggots.

my words are like my mother's
cells—furious & caustic & out of
time. i'm sure they'll be the death
of me too
         some day. until then

i'll gladly push two mLs of morphine
    beneath the tongue   of the afflicted
                as i did for her
   each day near   & until   the end
      because the last thing we

need is more pain.

On hearing the original *Jurassic Park* theme on piano in
Jurassic World & finally realizing how quickly time flies

even for dinosaurs—
& not just archaeopteryx
or microraptors. It flies
for the feathered, wingless
ones, too. Extinction never
did reptilian bodies *so good*
until now, re-engineering
all those species so sleek—
inauthentically scaled in
scarier greens & blues.

As a new child actor
pushes the doors open
to my memory, to a place
overgrown in island vines,
the soft notes of a piano suite
take me back to an old park
& a classic theme. To when
I was that boy's age, opening
things out of curiosity, young
arms lifted by the strings of
a triumphant crescendo.

But I can't hear the violins
anymore, just this piano's
high-pitched dream. & I don't
want to know the truth: scales
or feathers, sharp teeth
or dull molars. It took
a dinosaur & hundreds more
to show me how time passes
& comes back—its skin
smoother & in every color,
teeth sharper, ready to tear
apart anything that's left.

How to be strong

Truth is
I cry for weeks at a time.
Truth is
my cheeks tasted of saline
long before
my mother died, flushed & full
of something
like shame. My eyes needed to
let go.
I've been told not to break
a line
without forethought, but
melancholia doesn't
come on like that. Some of us
never learned
to smile & mean it.
If I could,
I wouldn't
be writing this poem, so I'm
gonna let
it feel like it doesn't need to be
a man, to be
brave. I'm gonna let this poem
lie
in the fetal position in its
apartment for days
not knowing
when
or if
it will move again.

Burnside Climb

Ruidoso, New Mexico

My hands cling to the wheel like it's a branch,
& this mountain is just another trunk to scale,

another thing we must hoist ourselves over
to look out from its crown. You are the pristine

diamond. I am a flawed emerald, which is to say,
to this mountain, we are both adornments.

We move higher & higher still, but I'm already
there—my lungs all kushy & smoke-stained

from a morning bowl. I should not be driving,
but you are not worried. You look to the burnside

of the Sierra Blanca—pines nearly indiscernible
in their black needle-less death. The aspens, too,

those boys all char-soaked & done up with ash.
It's hard to watch the young ones go, but we can't

call it needless, how the flame takes the old spruce
back into the earth, & lets this forest grow again.

We reach a locked gate & park. The hike up
to the lookout sores my lungs & all my soft edges,

slack & full of winter's sloth. All I see is shadow,
trunk after trunk an effigy, what the fire leaves

behind in its climb. You wait several yards ahead—
sleeves rolled & hand shading your face—looking.

Here's where the flames stopped: the half-burned
pine, the aspen un-singed, the spruce still ever-

green. Here's where I catch up to you, where we
follow the white of thriving aspens up to the peak.

How these boys up here must have quaked to
the crackling of barkskin, how their blond leaves

must have flickered all night in the light of nearby
fire. How my lungs feel like those rings within them

now—here, but shaken. Or like us for that matter,
remembering what it is to burn without the flames.

IV

deciduous qween, IV

of a tree or shrub, relatively broad-leaved,
rather than needlelike or scalelike

A boy once called me a beech leaf—
too straight-veined & sharp around
the edges to love, he said. Clearly,

he was no dendrologist. But guapo,
you know. You watched me fall from
a birch tree. Picked me up all torn

& dusty—another fragile dying thing
the world couldn't hold onto anymore.
My grooves, they aren't unswerving,

& I've never been able to commit
to the curves of my own body, how
stretch marks bloom from my love

handles like sanguine veins ready
for autumn, ready for this flesh to
turn color and fall from my bones.

I've got a broad-leaved base. It sags
a little, hangs heavier than in those
twinkish spring days of my youth

when it took less than a stiff breeze
to send me fluttering dizzy-headed
to some new resting place.

↙

We call the broad flat part of a leaf
its blade, or lamina. It cuts through
the wind, rustles with the soft chime

of a knife when blown against other
keen-green & dangling things. The boy
was right about my edge, I'll give him

that. I'm still a jagged-toothed blade—
the serration of a breadknife that opens
up those soft & most delicate loaves

like a prayer, like every slice is the body
of Christ. But I worship carbohydrates,
& the only body I've opened with a blade

is my own—flesh so full of yeast & flour
it pulls my skin apart, brings rise to my
leaf-bottomed jeans. How does a toothed

edge shape a body? One sacramental
mouthful at a time. This is my blade
broken for you. Remember me.

⤳

My father says I used to have such
a natural smile—pristine white teeth
& cheeks full of something like joy.

What happened? he asks. *I started to wear
my shame like a muzzle*, I say, to hide
the shiny edges of my lamina. Maybe

I like to be bound. Maybe I need you
to fold me along my midrib vein, gently
fasten the toothed jaw of this birch leaf

closed. Maybe there's a dimension
somewhere within me that must be
contained. Let's call that place *truth*.

⤴

The boy never told me I have a booty like
a thick-ass birch leaf. Others did. I still just
want to do the leafshutter with the evening

breeze, to make every ounce of my round-
bottomed blade shake & jiggle in a whirl-
wind of drums & bass. That's the truth,

let's go there. Make me grin & you can see
everything this body has ever been in my
sharp, broken smile. Feel it in the soft

dissonance of white scars, the ones that
spider around just above my waist, webbed
etchings of all the flesh that has come & gone.

Guapo, you aren't the first to touch me, to trace
your fingers through the empty grooves that
bloom from my ribs like ridges of symmetrical

leaf-skin. Maybe you'll be the last. Unfold me.
Rub me into nothing in your palms. I'm ready
to turn to ash, as long as it's in your hands.

Hot Shit
after Chen Chen

In winter, he taught you to love your shit,
that everything coming out of your body
is perfect, & you can touch that beauty if

you want. You understand it is all about
love by the end, how you hope someone
will handle your mess like it's still a part

of you worth protecting. Remember all of
those times it wasn't about love? The one
man who looked down at the small fleck

on his cock afterwards, said *That's fucking
disgusting*. You just stared blankly at him,
wondered what he used his asshole for.

You said the same thing to your first,
& it was about love that time. Remember
the empty feeling in your belly when you

saw it on yourself? Of course you do. You
still feel bad, want to apologize to every love
you've ever wronged, but you're getting older.

Your insides have only ever known a hollow
shame you've tried to fill with nameless men.
Know that I only say *you*, because I'm scared,

because I've heard it's bad to be too wrapped
up in the first person, because I hear too many
people describe other people's words as shit

lately, & I don't speak up. I don't say we can
all be some kind of hot shit. I just stare blankly
& remember it's all about love in the end.

I imagine how someone must have fucked
those words free. *Give me more of that shit.*
I'll hold that shit in my hands all night.

the power(bottom) is yours
for Captain Planet

I wanted you then—
all the silver-blue & crystalline

waves of muscle washing over
your body. Your hydropowered

biceps, turbine thighs, washboard
abs. I imagined my tongue gliding

through every trough, pausing
on each crest. You were the world

in my child eyes. Even now,
that green mullet has me crying

O Captain! my Captain! So I guess
I've always loved your planet.

Just call me Ma-ti—all heart
with a big gay monkey on my back.

Was it always so obvious? Did those
Planeteers see him sitting there

before I even knew? It's strange how
shame can change the climate of our

cheeks. How it tastes like petrol
when it leaks from my veins.

You always said, *The power is yours*,
but I want to give it back to you.

This ring glows heavy on my hand.
It's all earth & fire, wind & water,

but no love left in this drowning world.

All Afternoon

Yesterday, I built a glory hole, but no one
came, so I knelt alone—without acclaim—
my eyes on the clean tile floor, the wall un-
stained. What's a boy to do with such shame,
kneeling hollow-jawed in a duct-taped frame?
I crooned *A hole is a hole* all afternoon—
a sinful hymn to fan some flamer's flame.
There was no pilgrimage, no semen monsoon
strewn hard-pressed against that holy wall.
Just an empty arc, an unanswered call. Blame
anonymity. But we'll make this stall
a relic today; I've got to untame
your body. So come on, lean in, lay claim.
When you can't see the face, it's all the same.

**haiku for my first boyfriend
on his twenty-eighth birthday**

queer. another year.
my how all the years (and queers)
have loosened your rear.

I grew up wanting

to fuck my superhero, bend him
over, cape over face, & let him feel
something for once. Clark, baby,

you left those tortoiseshell rims on
the nightstand, your want the only
pulsing kryptonite that kept you

from coming too soon. Red boot tips
to sky, eyes swallowing universe as
it swallowed us both whole. It didn't

take x-ray vision for them to see right
through us. Your invincibility buried
under a baggy jacket & a high-pitched

voice. My desire to strip all that away—
a growing weakness for curves like yours,
for a strength alien to me. Somewhere

beneath the s-curl of your yellow shield,
a part of you needed to lift us up, to save
the planet crumbling around us, but you

always did your best work on your back,
or against the wall, so you let the world
burn that day. We watched hellfire rain

& brimstone through the open window
while you taught me to build a fortress
from my solitude. I kept your red speedo

for a souvenir, left you your belt & blue
tights, those leather boots hovering
toward the door. I kept the cape, too.

Just a little stained something to hold onto,
to remember the mess we made & the ones
who expected so much more from us.

Quaking Aspen,
or dendrophilia

naked boy
two hundred years young
winter stripped you—
wig gone
blond leaves blown
into the valley

you are a smooth one
now
bark slick as
winter's icy lick
tonguing your

tremblebranch
& barkquiver
until you come
again—flourish
of green sheen
budding from
your white skin

the years in dark
streaks across your
thick trunk

i feel your weak
sway today

let my hot breath
make you flicker
this morning—
a flame on our ridge
beneath this
sallow-hazed
dawn

bury my purple
lips
in your light
fading
bark

Jazz June

I. *Urban Dictionary says*

it's slang for doing the nasty,
like a sweet saxophone moan:

summertime & the brass is easy
& I feel good & I just want to be

easy with you. Well, I want to be
something nasty too, so give me

the name. Call me Jazz June,
& I'll be a queen as long as life

is this song—my heart a sprig
of clover. Listen to its petaled beat

as it sprouts from my shaved chest
draped in Ella's sequined shimmer.

Blossoms in my wig like Billie, so this
body feels close to a woman, again.

No blackface; this isn't that kind
of show. Drag is about the look

& the song, so put some Nina on.
Play me Etta & Sarah Vaughan

'cause this boy likes to sway low.
I'll read Gwendolyn real cool, real

slow; this is that kind of show.
Some nights we just need a poem

or a song, especially in Texas
& Mississippi.   Goddam.

II. *sweet, soft things*

I'm lying on the shag carpet in my grandparents' living room,
threads fraying in all the shades from brown to green, yellowed
& golden & in between, like Texas sod in late June—parched
& dying. I'm thirsty too, for a dream to speak to, to call my own.
This is that dream. From the dream's kitchen, apples simmer in
cinnamon, the sour flesh of Granny Smiths bubble in a sweet
earthen spice. Soon the apples will soften, like the woman over
the stove, her red curls thinner than in those photos on the wall.
Same color though, fiercely bright & aflame. Nanny stirs with
some fire too, dips her shoulders to that Boogie Woogie Bugle
Boy. I'm eight, so I still think the Andrews sisters can sing. True
they've got some brass, but no slow moan. Goddamn, it's been such
a jazzless June. Until she comes for me with that earthen tune on
the radio, at last. Etta's voice croons on, so I know Nanny's still
groovin', with a deeper lean now 'cause she sure ain't turning that
dial. I spread my fingers wide, bury them in the carpet. They are
flames from the friction, dying to press their heat to something
smooth & sweet, to fill the empty spaces of my body with summer
& this slow song, to press upon my cheek the thrill of a soft thing
burned. I don't know if Nanny's really moving along to that slow
simmer of percussion, to that stovetop beat, but those apples sure do
smell sweet. Someday, I'll be a sweet, soft thing too—a tender fruit
that tastes like home. But this is just a dream where I press my palms
into the carpet like a bone-dry lawn, where I reach for a woman's
brawny voice & let my hips sing along, where all my flames can touch
are those dead or dying things that make a boy's little body move.

III. *Jazz June used to thin gin*

before I changed my name & took
to the stage, back when I was just a boy
thirsty for something to change my state

of mind. I would go over to your house
when your parents were overseas, palms
sweaty & heart pulsing like a trombone's

heavy breath before Etta's voice comes in,
& she just wanna, & I just wanna be easy
with you. I remember how you'd empty

enough from each bottle—like Hendrick's
or Tanqueray or Bombay Sapphire—so we
could forget what we both really wanted,

or maybe we'd remember. You joked about
putting your lips around me. I just laughed
& watched the way your body filled those

jerseys & shorts to the brim with something
worth wanting. I just wanna, I just wanna,
but we'd just fill the bottles back up with

water, 'cause some poisons are too strong,
too dangerous. I learned to dilute those urges,
the ones from the empty spaces of my body.

I just drank until I could forget, until I could
listen to how she didn't want me sad & blue,
she just wanna, she just wanna. Me, too.

IV. *My daddy had a trumpet*

I never heard him play.
Found it in a velvet case—
rusty brass bent & buoyed
into some pitchless thing.
He let me wrap my mouth
around that instrument,
blow all kinds of ungodly
moans out its bell. From
my bedroom, from out back,
I'd raise all kinds of brassy
hell. He showed me how to
empty a full water key too,
how to press my finger to a
curved clip & watch the spit
drain from the valve. Yes,
my daddy wanted me to be
a sweet & tidy little thing;
he told me never to swallow
the fruits of my labor. Daddy,
I tried, but I just love to play
& play, & when I've got my
mind on that slow moan, those
notes, they sweat in the thick
bayou air, they taste like the
sweet sucrose of any fruit.

V. *The first time I jazzed June*

was in the front seat of a 1986 Ford pickup.
He parked between some baseball fields
just off the shore in La Porte. That summer
night was dark & silent & awful. All I could hear
was our breath, faint & light as trumpet gasps,
but no crescendo moan, only the sticky, humid
mess of our sweat & Texas heat. Before I left,

he told me it might have been better if I'd used
lube. *Even spit would work*, he said. I just thought
of that water key draining. The fruit of that
trumpet's labor, how my child lips made
a broken horn let go of a rusty song. All we
heard in the cab of that old truck was the soft,
quiet hum of waves on the shore. When I came

back from school the next summer, we met
again. Different truck. Same boy. This time
he reminded me to bring all we'd need to make
things go smoothly. That June heat made our
flesh so limber, & we both made something like
music that afternoon—a reprise of a softer tune,
first so slow & low, then faster with more moan.

I still don't remember his name. Let me call him
Jazz 'cause it was June, & our breath was hot-
mouthed, just wanting to be nasty on a smooth
neck, an open ear. He laid there & asked, *Do you
think you can go again?* I just sang, *Again, again.*

VI. *Urban Dictionary says*

it's something we do after we
thin gin & before we die soon,

like a swan song, or Billie's last
recording—the ones that left her lips

too soon. Where does our last breath
blow? I'm still here, a flicker of silver

heels onstage, but I've seen thinner days.
You can feel them in the fraying threads

of this corset, in my love handles' soft
flesh uncinched after the show. But while

I'm up there, running my palms down
my shaved thighs with the friction

of a child's fingers through shag carpet,
I still hear an earthen tone,

a deep dirge moan from the grave.
I know that's where I'm heading too,

but I wanna stay & shake the thick
bayou air, smell the bay through

a cracked window. I wanna fuck
a time, until we fill those days with

song. I just wanna, I just wanna
move & groove with you.

Note: "Jazz June" is inspired by language from Gwendolyn Brooks' "We Real Cool"
& lyrics from Ella Fitzgerald's "Summertime," Nina Simone's "Feeling Good" &
"Mississippi Goddam," Etta James' "I Just Want to Make Love to You" & "At Last,"
Billie Holliday's "All of Me," & the Andrews Sisters' "Boogie Woogie Bugle Boy."

Straight Boy

who hurt you? Who told you
      you had to be a man & nothing
more? I can see it in your eyes,
      a kind of suffering, like fear
of being something less than
      your father. Don't worry,
straight boy, I'm not going
      to touch you, I'm not going
to leave you lying there
      if you fall. I know the weight
of expectation, how it pulls
      you to your knees & tells you
you're nothing if you can't
      stand on your own again. I know
it's not easy, straight boy.
      How you want to hum along
to show tunes, even when
      you're sober, how you want
to stretch your legs over
      your head like all the limber
ladies around us, their backs
      on their yoga mats. Just let go.
I tried to be you once, to hold
      onto the hopes of the ones who
made us. Straight boy, just fold
      into who you are. It's gonna ache
in the flesh & the bone, in your
      hips where you hold your past
& your pain & your truth.
      Ease into that pain, straight
boy, & be good. Just be good
      to those girls.

V

deciduous qween, V
of plants and shrubs, shedding foliage at the end of the growing season

Will I remember how to move without emeralds,
without boas green as leaves wound around every
branch of this body? Summer is a gown, a canopy
of stems & blades that rustle to *The Elm Tree Hustle*
like a windy song over swaying hips, or a slow pose

that's all eyes & puckered lips. Summer hides those
parts of me that sprouted in early spring—rice-filled
hose knotted into C cups, foam pads that bloomed
some hips from a girthy trunk. Truth, like the wind,
is an invisible thing, but you can see it in the leaves'

gentle flicker, in a drag qween's heavy wrists arched
toward the spotlight—silver rings & press-on nails
glistening in summer heat. Truth: I am most fulfilled
when I move in another name, when I cinch & shave
the excess of my body, bury it beneath a sequined

sheen. Call me Twiggy. Call me Jazz June. Call me
Sharon Stoned. Call me anything but a man's name
because I was never a gospel. I'm all branch & blade
& cool summer shade until the show ends & autumn
air settles in, blows layers of foundation & concealer

from my cracked skin, my wrinkled bark. This is how
an identity lingers, how it floats like a powdered cloud
across a fiercely rusted sky, or dissipates in a faux fog
over an empty stage. One winter evening, you'll find me
standing naked in the woods, jewelry mounds of silver

shine & diamond rinds all around me like kindling—
those earrings & necklaces & bracelets that still cling
to the warmth of the spotlight. You'll watch me sway
& creak in the frosty air, branches reaching for those
ornaments that will always make a dark stage shimmer.

make-believe queen bees

Many a gay has played Beyoncé for a day,
a night really. We drag ourselves on stage
& reach for revenge in those bills—ones
& fives we tuck under the seams. Tuck
like everything else between our thighs.

Down in the bayou, my fairy drag mother
once wove a wig into my hair, glued fierce
lashes to my lids, & layered my face with base
after a close shave. Beneath my eyes, shadows
shimmered like green reeds all wet & wispy

on the water's edge. I poured rice in nude hose,
tied two knots for C cups so the boys could cop
a more natural feel—as though these qweens
would know the difference. Like the beaver
on a willow's girthy trunk, I cinched my love

handles in a duct-tape corset—soft white flesh
all sticky silver shine squeezed into red sequin
hot pants & a bustier—then stomped down each
step to that stage in six-inch stilettos. *Bootylicious.*
I knew my audience, how they'd watch me,

bite by bite, swallow that pb & j on stage.
They weren't ready for *that* jelly, nor the truth
of my thickening trunk, my saggy bark. See,
those gays loved their twiggy qweens or their
funny girls stout like a coastal redwood, but

not always the in-between. Many of those gays
down in the bayou loved Beyoncé, until she put
on a black beret & draped herself in gold rounds
of ammo for a halftime show. See, you can't serve
a crowd what they expect. The lesson of the show

is in the reaction, how she disabused those qweens
of their whiteness, & we watched their glittered
nails cling to it. I know I will never be the Queen.
My body could never fill those cups, & I'd never
fit into leather hot pants these days. But I'm scared

of those qweens who love their trees the same way
the men before them did—the branches & the rope,
their bullets & their guns. How they wear golden
ammunition on stage, shiny in their faux emulation
of a Queen's body they will never own, yet long to.

how you go

*One day, it's finally **time**. The mother tree reaches the end of her life or **becomes ill**. The showdown **might** take place during a summer **storm**. As torrents of rain pour down, **the brittle trunk** can no longer support **the** weight of several tons of **crown,** and **it shatters**. As the **tree** hits the ground, it **snaps** a couple of waiting **seedlings**. The gap that has opened up in the canopy **gives** the remaining members **of** the kindergarten the **green light**, and they can **begin** photosynthesizing to their **heart's content**. **Now** their metabolism gets into gear, **and** the trees grow sturdier **leaves and needles that** can withstand and metabolize bright light.*

—Peter Wohlleben

One day,
time becomes
ill,

might storm
the brittle
trunk.

The crown,
it shatters.

Tree snaps
seedlings,
gives of
green light.

Begin.

Heart's content
now, & leaves

& needles—

that bright
light.

rise again

*One day, it's finally time. The **mother tree** reaches the **end** of her life or **becomes** ill. The showdown might take place during a **summer** storm. As **torrents** of rain pour down, the brittle trunk can no longer support the weight of several tons of crown, **and** it **shatters**. As the tree hits the ground, it snaps a couple **of waiting** seedlings. The gap that has opened up **in** the **canopy** gives **the remaining** members of the kindergarten the green light, and they **can begin** photosynthesizing to **their** heart's content. **Now their** metabolism gets into gear, and the trees grow **sturdier leaves** and needles that can **withstand and** metabolize bright **light**.*

—Peter Wohlleben

Mother tree,
end.

Become summer—
torrents
& shatters

of waiting in canopy.

The remaining
can begin

their *now*,
their sturdier
leaves—

withstand
& light.

Beaver as Fairy Drag Mother

The trees are queer magic,
just look at them. Branches
arch to sky like soft-wristed
arms, hands twirl overhead
doing the leafshutter in the
evening breeze. I watch you
girdle a willow on the river's
edge. Beneath his thick green
weave of oval leaves, you
incise a waist
for him, you
make an
hour-
glass
of his
trunk—
one bite at
a time. His body
knows how the years
pass in rings within him,
but you carve through that
history, fashion him a tooth-
chipped corset. Then you scurry
down, and we watch that willow
sway. You wait for him to fall like
a drunk on a broken heel, for his
finger-leafed hands to press into
your riverbed. But I want this
diva to stay on his feet, to find
his balance with the wind
because sometimes, we need
to know a deciduous qween
can rise again, even after
she falls.

Plumage

You are on the phone with a customer service representative
or a restaurant's hostess or a potential employer, and they
mistake you for a woman again. They say *How can I help you,
ma'am?* as you ruffle your manhood to hide your high-pitched
plume. Then silence. Then *I'm so sorry, sir.* You wonder where
their regret comes from—how their embarrassment cracks
under the belief that emasculation is a cardinal sin. You are not
sorry anymore. All that hollow-stomach-dry-throat-wet-eyed
shame never changed how you can't control the shape or shade
or tone of your own body.

You know the western marsh harrier,
how he circles over wetlands—reeds and wisps of tall grass all
limber in the afternoon squalls. After two years, his feathers
turn dark brown, like a hen's—tufts of soft white upon his nape
and crown, light cream patches where the neck meets the wing
like it's still 1980 and feathered shoulder pads are all the rage.
You have his sallow yellow eyes, the only way to distinguish him
from the girls. Your voice—light and feathered in frailty—still
makes a sound, which is to say a hen's feather still cuts through
a sheet of wind, keeps a boy safe from a territorial cock, or two.

Ash Mama

I never called you *Mother Tree.*
May I nowthat your body
felled you—bark   sallow &
unfurling   from your hollow
bones? I saw   an emerald
ash borer   in your pancreas,
watched it loosen   your skin,
swallow you wholein one
month.   They said it would
take years. I never called
you   *Great Ash,* until
that's what you were—   dust
through   my fingers, filling
your   own   mother's   grave.
You never called me seedling,
your   weak-limbed boy—
frail-leaved &   thin-veined
in shadow.   Every tree needs
light,   every crown wants
to rise. We each wore   ours
differently. You died before
your mother.   No sun
for you,   no head in   star-
soaked canopy.   You kept me
alive   all the same,   until
they took you   away, left
your roots   in the ground,
bound to mine,   as if to say
*Grow, baby.   Reach, qween
boy. Let your crown   shine.*

Pando

for Irán

Mi amor, if you ever find yourself in Utah, look for Pando.
He is a Trembling Giant of a man, a Quaking Aspen of a tree.
Trust me, guapo, he knows the way I love you, how I'd spread
myself across one hundred acres, y seis más if need be, just to
give you un bosque—forty thousand trunks bound by the same
root. He's watched for eighty thousand years—before your god
walked this earth, before I buried mine in la tierra roja—how I
have waited for this lasting warmth, for the fires to stave off all
those skinny ass conifers. My heart is that clonal colony qween,
all thirteen million pounds of him, so I'm heavy for you too, my
love. All the suckering that got us here, every trunk a new root,
every root a new stem—you always make us rise again & again.
But maybe, you shouldn't go to Utah. Maybe seeing it there, all
old & heavy, tangled & coming out of the ground might just be
too real. They say the deer are too hungry, the bark beetles too
many, y root rot y cankers y lo demás. They say he's dying. How
could such a trembling, quaking giant rise & spread from a single
seed, then go? When he hollows, we will watch him fall trunk by
trunk until we bury him with our gods. I will tell you I adore you,
& you will ask, *Cuánto?* Hear me from my roots: *Mi amor, Pando.*

Bayou Baby

Hurricane Harvey, August 27, 2017

I.

When I was a child, I followed
a nutria up out the ditch, which
is to say we came from the same
place. My little hands smeared
muddy paw prints. My fingers
sunk into a water-swept incline.
I couldn't catch up to those buck
teeth, to that gray fur & snake
tail all awash in ocean rain. I said
Bye, you. I asked, *Where you going?*
I said *I'm scared of this water, too.*

II.

A woman rose from that soggy refuge—
orchid bloom & alligator teeth in her
dirty blonde hair. I called her mother.
I asked *Mama, where you been?* I said
I just wanna stay
by you.
Her eyes were the severe green
of that dangerous sky. Her body
was covered in ocean—water so
dirty it glistened like a silver gown.
She said *I'm gonna wear this storm out.*

III.

I learned to love a man the same
way I love the bayou—I got used
to his beauty. How much can you
take for me? How much will you
hold before you crest? I know you
just want to protect me. *I can't stay.*

IV.

There are two dried petals & thirteen teeth
on my daddy's mantel. He just sits at
home alone, waiting for the dirty water
to rise, to bring all that death to his
front porch. He'd welcome it inside too,
if he didn't love sitting in the rain so much.
& he'd leave if he could walk on water,
if he had somewhere else to go.

V.

There's a tuft of gray fur atop the fence
out back, a thin-scaled tail that hangs &
dips in the silver flow. A voice escapes
those buck teeth. *Where you going?* it asks.
Bye, you.

NOTES

"Hippocampus, or If I were a boy" is in conversation with Ada Limón's poem "How to Triumph Like a Girl."

"here & there": *Castilleja indivisa* is commonly known as Texas Indian paintbrush.

"Jazz June" is inspired by language from Gwendolyn Brooks' "We Real Cool" & incorporates lyrics from Ella Fitzgerald's "Summertime," Nina Simone's "Feeling Good" & "Mississippi Goddam," Etta James' "I Just Want to Make Love to You" & "At Last," Billie Holliday's "All of Me," & the Andrews Sisters' "Boogie Woogie Bugle Boy."

"Hot Shit" is in conversation with Chen Chen's poem "Winter."

"how you go" & "rise again" are both erasures which use language from Peter Wohlleben's *The Secret Life of Trees*.

"boundary // fluidity" incorporates quotes & information from Brendan Borrel's article "Ghosts of the Rio Grande" & Collin Schultz's article "Nearly 6,000 Migrants Have Died Along the Mexican-U.S. Border Since 2000" as interludes between each section of the poem.

"cactus mouth": *Opuntia macrocentra* is commonly known as purple pricklypear cactus, & *Opuntia macrocentra kush* refers to an imagined strain of marijuana from West Texas.

"Pando," Latin for "to spread out," is a clonal colony of a single male *Populus tremuloides*, or quaking aspen, thought to be one of the largest single living organisms alive on Earth.

"bodyslam glam" is inspired by Cassandro & all of the exóticos who perform lucha libre in drag. It incorporates research from William Finnegan's "The Man Without A Mask."

BIOGRAPHICAL NOTE

Matty Layne Glasgow was runner-up for the *Missouri Review*'s 2017 Jeffrey E. Smith Editors' Prize and finalist for *Nimrod*'s 2018 Pablo Neruda Prize. His poems have been nominated for the Pushcart Prize and Best of the Net anthologies and appear in the *Missouri Review, Crazyhorse, Collagist, BOAAT, Muzzle,* and elsewhere. He lives in Houston, Texas where he teaches with Writers in the Schools and adjuncts his life away.